Please Don't Kill
All the Poets

Palewell Press

Please Don't Kill All the Poets

Poems by Adnan Mohsen

Please Don't Kill All the Poets

First edition 2024 from Palewell Press,
www.palewellpress.co.uk

Printed and bound in the UK

ISBN 978-1-911587-79-8

All Rights Reserved. Copyright © 2024 Adnan Mohsen. Except for reviewers who may quote brief passages in a review, no part of this publication may be reproduced or transmitted in any form or by any means, without permission in writing from the author. The right of Adnan Mohsen to be identified as the author of this work has been asserted by him in accordance with the Copyright, Designs and Patents Act 1988

The cover design is Copyright © 2024 Camilla Reeve
The front cover painting is Copyright © 2024 Yahya Al-Sheikh, alsheikhyahya@gmail.com
The back cover photo of Adnan Mohsen is Copyright © 2024 Adnan Mohsen

A CIP catalogue record for this title is available from the British Library.

Acknowledgements

The translators would like to thank Adnan Mohsen for sharing his work with us and for his generous help with bringing these poems into English.

Thank you to the painter, Yahya Al-Sheikh, for offering the beautiful work from his collection that we have used on the cover and for his design insights.

We would like to thank Palewell Press for publishing this collection and inviting us into its community of writers.

Contents

Translator's Introduction	1
I Cry Alone in the Labyrinth	3
Memory	4
Deposits	5
Two wishes	6
Another wish	7
Education	8
Chants	9
Lapse of Memory	10
Missing childhood	11
Particularity	12
Another Confession	13
Third confession	14
Late admission	15
Orders	16
Habits	17
Losses	18
Modern Day Adam	19
Consideration	20
Mesopotamians	21
Noah	22
Origin of Mankind	23
Miracles	24
Photograph of Iraq	25
Ironica	26

Write as You Wish	27
Rascals	28
The Commandments	29
Lenin	30
Intentions	31
Bottom line	32
Differentials	33
Labyrinth	34
The Know It All	35
Paradise	36
Path	37
Rule	38
The Ruins	39
The Will	40
Stars for All Times	41
Talent	42
Exclamation Mark	43
Last Confession	44
Many Voices for One Throat	45
Poetry	46
Stenography	47
Cemetery	48
Another Wish	49
Habits	50
Virtual Return	51
What is Said and What is Not Said	52

The Years of Embargo	53
If	54
Finding Homeland	55
Reason	56
No Reason	57
Mirror	58
The Past	59
Mistakes	60
Long Distance	61
Nostalgia / And So On	62
Meeting	63
Waiver	64
Poetic Manifesto	65
Letters to Gudea	66
Letter 18	67
Letter 22	68
Letter 40	69
Letter 93	70
Letter 94	71
Letter 98	72
Letter 102	73
Letter 113	76
Letter 114	77
Letter 119	78
Letter 120	79
Adnan Mohsen Biography	80

Dr Anba Jawi, Translator/Editor Biography   81
Catherine Davidson, Translator/Editor Biography   82

Translator's Introduction

Adnan Mohsen was born in Baghdad in 1955, and has lived in Paris since 1981. He has published five poetry collections in Arabic. He has also translated a collection of Malcolm de Chazal poems as well as a book of essays about surrealism from French to Arabic and an anthology of Iraqi poets from Arabic into French.

I agreed to translate Adnan's poems into English while waiting at Conflans Sainte Honorine station for the train to take us to Paris. I usually visit him every year and stay with his family for few days. His lovely wife Aube has become my friend and we have endless chats about novels and music. That evening I started choosing the poems from his collections. On the train coming back to London I finished the selecting. My selection was spontaneous and unrestrained.

Previously, I had translated English to Arabic but not the other way around. I knew I was stepping into an unknown territory. In the time since we started working on Adnan's poetry, Catherine and I translated another book, an anthology of Iraqi poems, *The Utopians of Tahrir Square.*

In London I started the process. Adnan's poems are glowing, abrupt, sudden, surprising, and unexpected. Full of metaphor and layered, yet they are economic and above all ironic. These two characteristics make Adnan's poems unique. You might think his poems are about daily things everyone encounters yet they are reflective poems, forcing you to look at the seemingly ordinary more thoughtfully.

The language is simple, flexible, readable, free from rhetoric, precise, concise, compact, iconic and intellectual. They lack the rhetorical clutter that can characterise some Arabic poetry. He has said to me he wants above all for his poems to be accessible.

He reaches for the reader rather than the reader reaching for him. He writes about his life experience without an ornate display of his deep knowledge, and writes his precise poems with unique imagination. His knowledge of French literature plays a role in refining his work.

He does not follow rigid styles or forms; he unleashes his poems and provides them with liberty to flourish. I asked him once about his poems. He told me they are surrealistic, cheeky, mocking and sometimes even nihilistic.

Critics have described his poetry as being like films where one single take can encompass an entire scene. They are concise but not innocent. In one line he expresses life greased with humour, a poet who has escaped from the poets' barracks. They tend to be simple and gentle, uncomplicated and unambiguous.

The poems that follow are selected from several different books. The section headings come from the titles and sub-sections of the following collections: *I Cry Alone in the Labyrinth, Many Voices for One Throat,* and *Letters to Gudea.*

It is a pleasure to introduce Adnan's poems to the English reader: simply, they offer an irony-scented fresh air.
It was a joy working with Catherine who understood Adnan's poems and edited them skilfully and sympathetically.

Dr. Anba Jawi, Translator

I Cry Alone in the Labyrinth

Memory

I don't remember exactly
when I last cried for a woman
but I clearly remember
the city gardens
standing for one-minute's silence
whenever I walked by them on my own

Deposits

oh friend
when you decide to die
please, I beg you
give me back the tears
I deposited
temporarily
in your handkerchief

Two wishes

if I was a painter
I would make you a cat in my painting
and when I'd stroke your back
with my fingers
we'd meow together
you in the painting
and I in my room far away

come,
let us cross the road together
you on the right side of the pavement
and I on its left
may whoever stumbles first
leave some of his last gasp
in his friend's pocket

Another wish

how I wish I lived
with a woman poet
we would divide
our duties equally
I could drink
and she could write
my poems for me

Education

I did not learn love
not at home
and not at school
but whenever
I fell into it
I figured it out right away
there are symptoms
unseen by the naked eye
I've seen them
I don't know how

Chants

I have a mouth good only for singing
that's why I look for the high points
to sprinkle my songs on peoples' heads

First song:

things are not equal in the dark

Second song:

everything I did not see yesterday
will be repeated in the days to come

Third Song:

I give them my last mask
but I worry about the mark
the remnants of my rust
will leave on their faces

Lapse of Memory

everything was arranged for the funeral
the Angel of Death was sitting on the sofa
friends were ready to list my virtues
suddenly he turned away from me
I forgot to die in return

Missing childhood

once my mother told me:
of all children you left my womb
without it ever occurring to you to cry
you were busy searching for your twin
the only one who knows where to place
exclamation marks and question marks
in your incomplete sentences

Particularity

I live only once
like all humans and their kind
loving more than one woman
and more than one man
I die several times a day

it is my habit to repeat my vices
except for insults –
no one deserves to be insulted twice

Another Confession

in the beginning,
I didn't tell her I was a poet
a suspicious word these days
I am a rascal, that's all
I can barely read and write
I don't know about women's
perfumes and hair styles
I don't care about eloquence
I know all about rhetoric
I am capable of saying the same thing
at any time, more than once
and each time with new zest

Third confession

on her way to the plains
she did not forget
to bury my umbilical cord
in her childhood fields

Late admission

there is only one flaw in my soul
it has no siren

Orders

I was born with fire
we lived together
grew up together
in obedience and disobedience
today I gave her my last order
go out
go out
I want to learn to walk alone in the dark

Habits

I forgot everything
lost interest in anything
except sitting on the doorstep
like my mother
when I came back home late
in the middle of the night

the difference between me and her
is that I forgot long ago
who I'm waiting for
and who is worth the wait

Losses

all my acquaintances are losers
if I was a sculptor
I would make a statue of loss
place it in the guest room
to welcome people on my behalf
while we were next door
falling into deep sleep

Modern Day Adam

I've created for more than one Eve
a perfect apple
and excellent teeth
to keep her munching
for as long as possible
while I am
in a corner of the bar
thinking only of you

Consideration

her parade
goes up the mountain
it's worth watching
I am on the foothill
I am also worthy of consideration
I am bringing wine
for those who
don't want to climb
for any reason

Mesopotamians

Noah

Noah
you idiot
why did it cross your mind
to take one pair of each couple
it was enough to take
two monkeys
two fish
two cats
and two mice
and from humans just you
there'd be no trace of you after you died
you would have saved us traveling from city to city
monkeys fish cats dogs and mice are preferable to us

Origin of Mankind

I know their ancestors from their actions
Mr Darwin made a big mistake
not everyone has a monkey grandfather
some are sons of dogs
some descendants of pigs
some the offspring of sheep
some come from a bunch of crocodiles
some jackals
some from the belly of chameleons
some are progeny of parrots
some come from the pedigree of Earuqub*
and we are among them
we chose the hearts of fish
that can beat only in our chests

Earuqub is a famous liar

Miracles

I can make wonders
to brush ants' teeth
manicure the nails of whales
invite fish to jog near the river
help the bird to rave
teach my dog to sleep standing up
and my cat to dance on her tiptoes
I can walk over water
I can create all possible miracles
but I can't cross the road
with you, my love, walking behind me

Photograph of Iraq

before they steal them
come with me
let's take a memorial photo
with the date palm trees

Ironica

Write as You Wish

write meter
or without meter or rhyme
be symbolist
be parnassianist
be futurist
be cubist
be dadaist
be surrealist
be metaphysical
be what you like
but write something that reminds us of you
when poetry crosses our mind

Rascals

Whenever I hear someone say
if memory doesn't fail me
I say to myself
I wish it would

And whenever I hear them say
let's hit two birds
with one stone
I put my hand on my heart
among them I don't see any bird but me
surrounded everywhere by their stones

Of the oddity of the soul
that no longer craves
or can be shamed

The Commandments

Don't kill all the poets please
leave a small sample
for the labs of the future
so that people know
a type of human
lived before them
who worked day and night
with souls like smoke-stacks
without wages
and for no reason

Lenin

Lenin!
save me my old friend
I no longer know
"what is to be done?"
do I wail with the wailers
for the homeland
or chase that lady
who pointed at me
with her finger
when I have no idea
what's going on in her head?

Intentions

when you arrive
I will stand behind you
watching God's angels
it might cross their mind
what is crossing mine

Bottom line

bottom line
whatever's read from right to left
and from left to right
and from top to bottom
and from bottom to top
and its meaning stays the same

Differentials

woman
even in a wheel chair
thinks about the future
and man
starts thinking about the past
as soon as he reaches twenty

when woman loves
she installs an early warning system in her heart
and when a man loves
he borrows his brain from any bird

Labyrinth

I laughed out loud
when I reached the maze
a philanthropist was waiting for me
in his hand a map
to show me my way
among us how many ignorant
we sons of the no man's land
we walk in the dark
we know all the paths
no need for a guide
or a compass

The Know It All

he knows what's happening on this globe
from Cape of Good Hope
to the Shifting Sands
and from Waqwaq* islands
to the Bay of Pigs
but he has no idea
what's going on in the head
of the wife sitting next to him

Mythical islands in Medieval Arabic literature

Paradise

I will definitely enter paradise
I checked my accounts

on the Lord's books
I have some life arrears
that are still owed me

Path

none of us know the path
that leads to our dreams
as for those leading to nightmares
we know them by heart
and each one of us can
reach them blindfolded

Rule

they say
we only live once

that's true
for those who live full lives
only the crazy would do that

the wise
live always half the time
and no more

The Ruins

we waited for the beautiful reconstruction
the destruction arrived immediately

I imagine that the grandchildren
of the grandchildren of our grandchildren
will still be waiting for the beautiful like us
with equal idiocy

The Will

oh Lord
we don't need to fear each other
I will not fear you
you are forgiving and merciful
for your part
don't be afraid of me
I'm no good at punishing others

Stars for All Times

some
see the stars only at night
others
see them at all times

Talent

a woman poet with no talent:
the same as those
who sleep with a man
and don't enjoy it
and the untalented poet?
the same as those
who sleep with a woman
and are the only ones
to experience pleasure

Exclamation Mark

my questions need
countless
question marks

and one exclamation mark
a little taller than me
is no measure of my surprise

Last Confession

I don't fear death at all
all I fear
after my death is that
they might lower the price of wine and cigarettes
and I will miss the train as usual

Many Voices for One Throat

Poetry

I write for a simple reason
for my friends to know
I am still alive
and have illusions
still left on my ledger

all I want in my life
is to write a couple of lines
to leave on my gravestone
so when passers-by
come to the cemetery
those who do not know me
can see the headstone and say
here rests a poet

Stenography

all I have sought in my life
is to reduce my pains
with a few lines
let's say
the number of the fingers on one hand
then the pain expanded
so I hired the fingers of the second hand
then my toes
then family members' fingers
here I am looking at your fingers
with a wolf's eagerness in front of prey

Cemetery

during my youth
I didn't know the names of flowers
didn't care much about that
in front of me
was only one banner:
cemetery seats empty for all!
that was my homeland

Another Wish

how I wish
to lie and to believe all my lies
to fall asleep just once
before the city snores in its sleep

Habits

I may laugh twice
cry twice
if necessary
keep quiet twice
but when
I swear
I swear only once
nobody deserves to be sworn at twice

I have one wish
to be myself
dressed to the nines
with full mental capacity
the third leg
for everyone
trying to reach themselves
on foot

Virtual Return

I was born near a river
and near a river I will die
throw my remains in any river
I know the river will lose its way
perhaps it will lead me one day
back to where I left my waters

What is Said and What is Not Said

The Years of Embargo

I am dreading one thing
and one thing only
the last crumb of bread
stumbling in my mother's mouth
while others look on

If

if God were fair
He would ask Iraqis for forgiveness

Finding Homeland

Today I found a homeland
as beautiful as anything simple
where morning doesn't mock my night
women accept all of my follies
and a friend is determined
to divide all mistakes by two

Reason

you might cry for no reason
and laugh for any reason
you might love a woman and not know the reason
you might write for no reason
and live and die without the slightest reason
but when the smoke is rising from your head
don't bother to find out the reason

No Reason

the moment I was thinking of crying
I looked at the mirror
I saw a man laughing
we're now making each other laugh
and we have no idea why

Mirror

whenever I look in the mirror
I see a man who looks like me
but with a better sense of humour
maybe he's lost his memory

The Past

every night
I put the past down next to me and sleep
in the morning we exchange greetings and some trivia
today it wasn't in its usual place in bed
whispering in a faint and sad voice
hasn't the time come
to put me out of my misery?

Mistakes

Apollinaire was asking
for forgiveness for his mistakes
what a disappointment
we are his descendants
walking the length and breadth of earth
expanding our praise of them

Long Distance

you in the distance
any distance
don't be surprised
if I say I love you
although I haven't met you
I don't know
if you're a man or woman
young or old
it's enough that you are far away
to love you
for years I didn't do love
except from a distance

Nostalgia / And So On

Meeting

yesterday
I had a dream I was in Baghdad
I kissed her hand and cried
she looked at me and exclaimed
oh God, how much we've changed

Waiver

take everything
money
status
celebrity
children
memories
homelands
take all the streets
and leave me the potholes
to guide me on my way
take all the stars
and leave the night for me alone
take the excesses of the day
and the surplus of blood
leftover hopes
take everything
and leave for me
plenty of white paper
and one hand
to write my poems
and wave to my sweetheart
from a distance

Poetic Manifesto

we don't need huge armies
and intercontinental weapons
take this homeland
we don't want it
we've had enough of your defeats
and we are bored of our losses
take what no longer resembles us
we will not continue in its image
divide it between yourselves
like sharing whores in a brothel
leave for us only women who believe in love
and men who believe in themselves
perhaps one day we will return from our deaths
and rise from the ashes of our souls

Letters to Gudea

Letter 18

The city circus was
looking for a clown,
and I was unemployed.
I knew my talents.
I laugh for a reason
and I cry for the same reason.
I said to myself,
"I will make them piss themselves laughing."
I submitted my application, sent my CV
and they gave me a try-out.

In my first show,
as soon as I opened my mouth,
and the audience saw my face
and the plumes of smoke swirling around me
they took their handkerchiefs out of their pockets
and began to wave at each other, in tears.

Gudea is an ancient Sumerian king who married into the royal family of Lagash and ushered in a golden age. There are 120 Letters in the book; we have chosen a selection.

Letter 22

When
for the first time
I told a girl I love you
my face changed colour
my hands shook
my heart was beating strangely

Her name was Shereen *
I was told she had gone
to visit her family
and never returned

Since then
I have told many girls I love them
the colour of my face
remained unchanged
and my hands were steady

But,
whenever I see a man
ashen, his hands shaking
I say to myself
he has done it, pal
he declared his love to a woman
who went to visit her family
and never came back

Shereen is a Kurdish female name meaning pretty, the poet is referring to the bombing of Kurdish villages in Kurdistan, northern Iraq.

Letter 40

This morning
I saw what a sleeper sees in his sleep
my mother stepped out from her grave
went to the town market
bought a cell phone
to write quickly as usual:

Here my son is a world you would like
no need for any more emotions
no need for extra time
no need for money
I personally don't want you with me
no one is missing anyone
visiting each other is forbidden
and, I am happy to tell you,
we are all naked
our possessions are for everyone
I am sure
you will achieve your dream
of equality among humans
when you are our guest

Letter 93

Our good neighbour
her husband told her
don't worry
God is with us
after a week
her first born son
was killed in the Iraq Iran war
after years
her second son died
in the Kuwait invasion
after years
Bush's missiles landed
on her only daughter's house
and when she sold her bedding
during the sanctions
she shouted at her husband
what would have happened
if God had not been with us?

Letter 94

We might die from hunger
or from thirst
or even from love
but
from the beginning of humanity
no one has died of shame
even for a laugh, for example

Letter 98

When Yasser Arafat married
I bought a car
we both were
expressing our frustration
in our own way
he from the cause
and I from my feet

Letter 102

I wrote to Galileo Galilei
I said to him:
how foolish you were my friend
you should have plied all the priests
with wine till their heads spun
then they would have seen for themselves
that the earth turns

I said to Sisyphus:
I have never seen a man more idiotic
you wasted your time going up and down
for a rock
we hold you as an example
for anything we can't do
you should have thrown the rock into the valley
and gone back to them
after you had a drink or two
and told them you couldn't locate the mountain

I said to Borges:
my friend
I don't know if you read
before you go to sleep
or recall the last colour
or last friend you saw
but I tell you
as if I see you now in front of me
before you turn off the light
and close your eyes
you lead the darkness to its dignity
and restore its reputation
for every bird builds its nest
blindfolded

I called Gilgamesh
what's wrong with you?
Enkidu is dead!
so what?
Today
death is a national sport
and when friends die
we forget them
on our way to the cemetery

And you Penelope,
your waiting for Ulysses
warmed our hearts
and satisfied us all
you should have
written a complaint to Homer
he made you weave for twenty years
and denied you the ability
to write your own poem

I told Jesus
you know the strength
of affection between us
but let me rebel against you
next time someone
hits you on the left cheek
don't turn the right
they get into the habit
of hitting us, my friend

And you Voltaire
I need you the most
I don't want you to pay with your life
for my opinions
the story of opinions ended with us
we recited Al-Fatiha over it
I want you to come
to defend my wish
to raise my glass
to whoever I want
whenever I want

Letter 113

It was for God
or to whom it may concern
to ask for the blessing of drawing talent
I would have drawn her piece by piece
without any arrangement
put her head in my bedroom
her hands under the table
her fingers on the top of my desk
her lips not far from my mouth
her feet near the window
so that
whenever I am alone
pacing the house back and forth
she can besiege me from all directions

Letter 114

Two days ago
I ran into Lautréamont
I shouted at him
haven't I told you
your songs shatter my nerves
and set fire to my eyes
here I am
sleeping at my house
like an uninvited guest

Letter 119

Iraqi woman
either housewife or poet
and Iraqi man
either killer or killed
other than that
we are a great nation

We invented *Gagik**
without international aid
and dug for onions in no man's land
we developed chickpea cookery
we import leeks and parsley
and if necessary
we are content with radishes

we know all of God's names
and none of the names of flowers
we tolerate summer without electricity
and winters without our darlings

here we are a great nation
without knowing it
our lives are not precious
and the blood in our veins
is easy to spill
and for many reasons
we have gotten used to offering
our lives and blood to anyone

*cucumbers with yogurt and garlic

Letter 120

In the end
I wished to say to you
I am good
very good
all that I lack
is peace of mind
no more no less
still I have a last wish
to be a cat
with seven lives
gambling with five of them
day and night
I will keep one to help me write to you
as for the last one
I will use it to see
friends and family from afar

I found out from home
there is no place for me
I found out from exile
my only place is home

So, Grandfather
like a man who calculates his debts
at the end of the month
I have no home
and no exile

Adnan Mohsen Biography

Adnan Mohsen was born in Baghdad in 1955. After finishing his first degree at Baghdad University in 1978, he was forced to leave Iraq due to his stand against the dictatorship. He moved to Lebanon, Syria, Algeria and Libya, arriving in Paris 1981. He received his doctorate from the University of Jusseiu. He works at the Louvre.

He published *Memory of Silence*, his first French poetry collection in 1994, followed by *et cetera* 1995; *Texts about others* 1996 and *like this* as a dual edition in French and Arabic in 2000.

In Arabic he has published *Many Voices for One Throat* 2016; *I Cry Alone in the Labyrinth* 2016; *Definition* 2016 and *Letters to Gudea* 2018.

In 2016, Adnan's interest in Surrealism led to the Surrealism Adventure, a collection of articles written by the pioneers of surrealism along with poems and activities he translated from French to Arabic. This was followed by the Surrealism Archives in 2019, a translation of his research into archival material focusing on surrealist explorations of sexuality.

He introduced Malcolm de Chazal to the Arabic reader by publishing a translation of his poems in 2018. He has introduced Iraqi and Arabic poets to French readers through his numerous translations from Arabic to French.

Adnan is married to Aube de Thiersant, the daughter of the Savoyard painter Jacques de Thiersant. They have two children, a son Adam and a daughter Amielle.

Dr Anba Jawi, Translator/Editor Biography

Born in Baghdad, Dr Anba Jawi studied Geology at the University of Baghdad, one of a generation of pioneering women geologists in Iraq, and gained her PhD from UCL London. She worked in the refugee sector for more than 20 years and was honoured with an MBE on the Queen's birthday list in 2004 for her services. Anba writes and publishes in Arabic and English. A chapter from her novel *The Silver Engraver* was included in the TLC *Free Reads Anthology* (2019) and two chapters were produced in a chapbook published by Exiled Writers Ink (2021). Together with Catherine Temma Davidson, Dr Anba Jawi co-translated and co-edited *The Utopians of Tahrir Square*, published by Palewell Press in 2022.

Catherine Davidson, Translator/Editor Biography

Catherine Davidson is an American living in London and a dual UK/US citizen. Her novel based on stories about her Greek mother and grandmother, *The Priest Fainted*, was a New York and LA Times notable book of the year. She is an award-winning poet with two pamphlets published in the UK. She teaches Creative Writing at Regent's University and is on the Board of Exiled Writers Ink, an organisation that supports and amplifies the work of refugee and immigrant writers. Her novel about apricot jam, genocide and memory, *The Orchard*, was published by Gemma Media in 2018. Catherine Davidson co-translated and co-edited *The Utopians of Tahrir Square*, published by Palewell Press in 2022.

Palewell Press

Palewell Press is an independent publisher handling poetry, fiction and non-fiction with a focus on books that foster Justice, Equality and Sustainability.
The Editor can be reached on enquiries@palewellpress.co.uk

www.ingramcontent.com/pod-product-compliance
Lightning Source LLC
Chambersburg PA
CBHW070313120526
44590CB00017B/2658